Kansas

BY ANN HEINRICHS

Content Adviser: Duane Johnson, State Librarian, Kansas State Library, Topeka, Kansas

Reading Adviser: Dr. Linda D. Labbo, Department of Reading Education, College of Education, The University of Georgia

COMPASS POINT BOOKS MINNEAPOLIS, MINNESOTA

Compass Point Books
3109 West 50th Street, #115
Minneapolis, MN 55410

Visit Compass Point Books on the Internet at *www.compasspointbooks.com*
or e-mail your request to *custserv@compasspointbooks.com*

On the cover: Castle Rock in Gove County

Photographs ©: Steve Mulligan, cover, 1; Shade of the cottonwood/Michael C. Snell, 3, 6, 7, 12, 29,
31, 32, 39, 40; Unicorn Stock Photos/James L. Fly, 5; Unicorn Stock Photos/Aneal Vohra, 9; Unicorn
Stock Photos/Andre Jenny, 10, 42; Unicorn Stock Photos/Eric R. Berndt, 11, 26; Hulton/Archive by
Getty Images, 13, 14, 15, 16, 17, 18, 19, 24, 33, 34, 41, 46; John Elk III, 20, 21, 22, 35, 36, 38, 43,
45, 47, 48 (top); Photo Network/Howard Rolsom, 25; Unicorn Stock Photos/Jim Shippee, 27; Photo
Network/Ehlers, 28; Robesus, Inc., 43 (state flag); One Mile Up, Inc., 43 (state seal); Robert McCaw,
44 (top and middle); Comstock, 44.

Editors: E. Russell Primm, Emily J. Dolbear, and Patricia Stockland
Photo Researcher: Marcie C. Spence
Photo Selector: Linda S. Koutris
Designer/Page Production: The Design Lab/Jaime Martens
Cartographer: XNR Productions, Inc.

Library of Congress Cataloging-in-Publication Data
Heinrichs, Ann.
  Kansas / by Ann Heinrichs.
    p. cm. — (This land is your land)
  Summary: Describes the geography, history, government, people, culture, and attractions of the state
of Kansas. Includes bibliographical references and index.
  ISBN 0-7565-0353-1 (hardcover : alk. paper)
  1. Kansas—Juvenile literature. [1. Kansas.] I. Title. II. Series.
  F681.3.H45 2003
  978.1—dc21   2003002343

Table of Contents

NOTE: In this book, words that are defined in the glossary are in **bold** *the first time they appear in the text.*

Welcome to Kansas!

Lydia Allen Budd rumbled across Kansas in a covered wagon in 1852. One day she wrote: "We have come ten miles today. Encamped on a small stream called Vermillion Creek. . . . There are as many as fifty wagons on this stream. . . . It looks like a village. The tents and wagons extend as much as a mile."

Lydia was one of thousands of **pioneers** on the Oregon Trail. Some stayed on the trail until they reached California or Oregon. Others stopped in Kansas. There, they built log cabins or sod houses. They made the sod houses from thatched grass and earth bricks cut from the prairie grass sod. They braved snowstorms, dust storms, and dry spells. In time, Kansas became the top wheat-growing state.

Kansas has had an interesting history. In the 1850s, it was called "Bleeding Kansas" because of fights over slavery. In the 1870s and 1880s, cowboys herded cattle to Dodge City and other Kansas towns. Dozens of movies and television shows recall those wild, lawless days.

▲ **A hay bale and barn in northeast Kansas**

Today, Kansas is not only a leading farm state. It's also a leader in making airplanes and airplane parts. Now let's explore Kansas—a super-modern state with an exciting past.

▲ The marker in Lebanon showing the geographic center of the country's contiguous states

Take a look at a U.S. map. Which state looks like it's right in the center of the country? If you picked Kansas, you'd be correct! The geographic center of the forty-eight contiguous, or connected, states is on a farm in Lebanon. It's the exact north-south and east-west midpoint. A stone marker in a nearby field marks the area's importance.

Kansas may be the "center state." However, it is considered a Midwest state. It lies between Nebraska, which is to the north, and Oklahoma, which is to the south. To the east is Missouri, and to the west is Colorado.

Most of Kansas is made up of flat or rolling plains. These plains were once the bottom of an inland sea. As the sea dried up, mineral-rich soil sank to the bottom. That soil makes Kansas the rich farming region it is today.

▲ Clouds roll across the plains of Z-Bar Ranch near Strong City.

Kansas's plains slope higher as you go westward toward Colorado. They're part of America's Great Plains. A few strange rock formations tower over the high plains in the far western part of the state. Northeastern Kansas is called the Dissected Till Plains. Over millions of years, rivers have worn high, rocky cliffs into the land. Many creeks run through the region's forested hills.

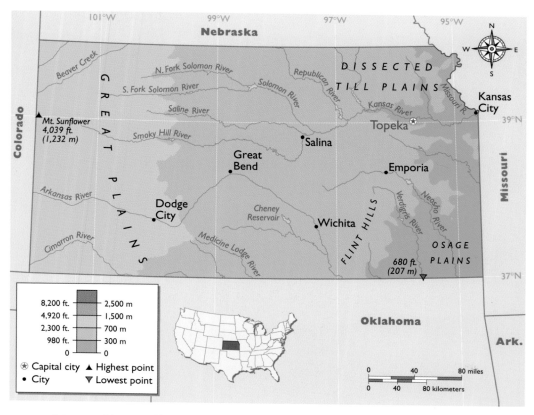

▲ A topographic map of Kansas

▲ **The Flint Hills in east-central Kansas**

The Flint Hills of east-central Kansas are great for grazing cattle. The cattle feast on the tall grasses growing there. The Osage Plains of southeast Kansas are low, rolling hills. Many valuable minerals lie underground in this area.

Two big rivers with several branches flow across Kansas. The Kansas River is in the northern part of the state. Kansans often call it the Kaw River. At Kansas City, on the state's eastern border, the Kansas joins the Missouri River. Lawrence and

▲ **The Arkansas River flows past Wichita.**

Topeka, the state capital, lie along the Kansas River. In the south is the Arkansas River. It runs past Wichita, Kansas's largest city.

Vast herds of buffalo, or bison, once grazed on Kansas's grassy plains. By the late 1800s, hunters had wiped out these herds. Deer now roam across the plains. Among the state's smaller animals are prairie dogs, coyotes, and raccoons.

Western Kansas is home to many ground-dwelling birds. They include quail, pheasant, and prairie chickens, or grouse. More prairie chickens live in Kansas than anywhere else in North America. The state also has an interesting and colorful variety of tree-nesting birds.

The sunflower, Kansas's state flower, is found throughout the state. Bushy plants called tumbleweeds grow in Kansas, too. When fall winds blow, they bounce and tumble across the plains.

Have you seen the movie *The Wizard of Oz?* Dorothy and her dog, Toto, lived on a Kansas farm. One day a tornado swept them away to a bizarre place called Oz. Dorothy could only say, "Toto, I've a feeling we're not in Kansas anymore." You may sometimes hear people say, "We're not in Kansas anymore." They mean that they're in a totally weird situation!

▲ **Sunflowers growing in east-central Kansas**

Tornadoes do sweep through Kansas. Blizzards, thunderstorms, and hailstorms come through Kansas, too. Why is Kansas so stormy? The answer is that the plains are so level. Winds can easily blow across them in both winter and summer.

Winters in Kansas are cold, and summers are warm. Northern Kansas is a bit cooler than the south. Southeastern Kansas gets the most rain and snow, while the far west is the driest region.

▲ **Snow covers a creek in Riley County.**

A Trip Through Time

Thousands of Native Americans once roamed the Great Plains. Those in Kansas included the Plains Apache, Kiowa, Arapaho, Cheyenne, Pawnee, Wichita, Osage, and Kansa, or Kaw. These Native Americans hunted buffalo for meat and **hides.** They also raised corn, beans, and squash and gathered wild plants. Some groups moved from place to place, following the buffalo herds. Others settled permanently in villages. They built homes out of thatched grass, buffalo hides, or bricks of prairie sod grass.

▲ Sharitarish was a chief of the Pawnee tribe, which hunted on Kansas's plains.

Spanish explorer Francisco Vásquez de Coronado was the first European to arrive in the area that is now Kansas. He entered this region in 1541. In 1682, France claimed a vast

▲ Coronado (on horseback) entered present-day Kansas in 1541.

area that included this land. The United States bought this land in 1803. Some of the land that would later become Kansas was still controlled by Spain.

The American explorer Zebulon Pike passed through this area in 1806. He described the region as desertlike and worthless for farming. In 1821, the explorer Stephen Long visited for the U.S. Engineering Corps. He created a map that named the region the Great American Desert. Because of these errors, people were confused for several years and thought this valuable region was a desert.

▲ **American explorer Zebulon Pike in 1805**

Traders and pioneers began heading west in long lines of

covered wagons. The Oregon and Santa Fe Trails were two famous routes through Kansas. Most travelers were headed for the western United States. However, some realized that Kansas was not such a desert after all. They decided to settle there and farm.

At that time, arguments about slavery were tearing the nation apart. Some Kansans were in favor of slavery, while others were against it. In 1854, Congress passed the Kansas-Nebraska Act. It created Kansas Territory. Congress also let new territories decide about slavery for themselves.

▲ **Camp Comanche, a trading camp on the Santa Fe Trail**

▲ Pro-slavery settlers killed antislavery settlers at Marais Des Cygnes in 1858. This was one of many conflicts that earned Kansas the name "Bleeding Kansas."

This seemed like a good idea at the time. It was a disaster for Kansas, though. People for and against slavery fought each other in bloody battles. Soon the territory was called "Bleeding Kansas." At last, in 1861, Kansas joined the Union. It entered as a free state, which is a state that did not allow slavery. However, the conflict over slavery led to America's Civil War (1861–1865).

In the 1870s and 1880s, many Kansans were raising cattle. New railroads shipped the cattle to markets in faraway states. Dodge City, Abilene, and other cities became important railroad centers. They were also called cow towns, or cattle towns.

Cowboys from Texas and other states led big cattle drives to Kansas. These cowboys got pretty wild. Outlaws roamed the cow towns, too. Lawmen such as Wyatt Earp and Wild Bill Hickok tried to keep order.

A religious group called the Mennonites settled in Kansas in 1874. They brought with them a hardy type of wheat called Turkey Red. This wheat flourished on the state's fertile plains. In time, Kansas became the nation's top wheat producer. Petroleum (oil), natural gas, and coal were discovered in Kansas, too. By the early 1900s, Kansas was an important mining state.

Kansans had a terrible time in the 1930s. Drought, or lack of rain, left farmland dry and parched. Then dust storms swept through, blowing **topsoil** away. At the same time, the nation's Great Depression left thousands homeless.

▲ **Wild Bill Hickok**

▲ **A dust storm approaches Elkhart in 1937.**

Manufacturing was a growing **industry** in Kansas, though. During World War II (1939–1945), Kansas supplied airplanes for the war. The state's wheat and minerals were valuable war supplies, too. After the war, Kansas farmers worked on new ways to protect their soil. They also developed **irrigation** using underground water.

Farming, natural gas, and manufacturing are important industries in Kansas today. Airplane manufacturing is the largest single industry and is larger than all of agriculture. However, each of these industries has had its ups and downs. State leaders are working hard to keep Kansas healthy and strong.

▲ The state capitol in Topeka

Topeka became Kansas's capital city when the state entered the Union in 1861.

Like other states, Kansas divides its state government into three branches—legislative, executive, and judicial. The national government is organized the same way. This system makes for a good balance of power. Each branch keeps the others from becoming too strong.

The legislative branch creates the state laws. Kansas's lawmakers serve in the state legislature. It is divided into two houses, or sections—a 40-member senate and a 125-member house of representatives. Voters elect their lawmakers from districts divided by population. That gives everyone an equal voice in the state government.

The executive branch works with the legislature to create the laws. Then it's responsible for carrying out those laws. Voters elect the governor to head the executive branch. The governor serves a four-year term. The secretary of state, attorney general, and treasurer are other elected officials.

▲ State lawmakers meet in the senate chamber of the state capitol in Topeka.

▲ Judges hear cases in the Chase County Courthouse in Cottonwood Falls.

Judges and their courts make up the judicial branch. A judge and the judge's jury of citizens listen to cases in court. Then they decide whether someone has broken the law. Kansas's highest court is the state supreme court. The governor appoints its seven justices, or judges. However, the voters decide later whether a justice can stay in office.

Kansas is divided into 105 counties. Voters elect county commissioners. They also elect a sheriff, county clerk, and

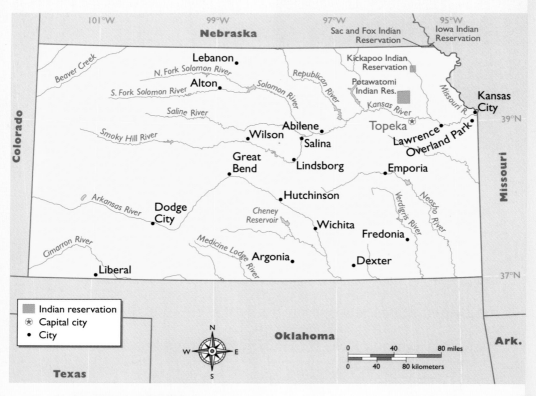

▲ **A geopolitical map of Kansas**

▲ **Kansan Dwight D. Eisenhower was the thirty-fourth U.S. president.**

other county officers. Both cities and counties in Kansas have home rule. That means they can make many government decisions themselves. Most cities elect a mayor and a city council. Some big cities choose to be governed by a group of commissioners.

Kansans are proud of their homegrown leaders. Dwight D. Eisenhower grew up in Abilene. As an army officer, he was promoted to the position of commanding general. He led the forces that won World War II. Following this success, he was elected the thirty-fourth president of the United States and served from 1953 to 1961. Robert Dole is another famous Kansan. He served in the U.S. Senate (1969–1996) and ran for president in 1996.

Kansans at Work

▲ Wheat fields cover much of Kansas.

Drive through Kansas and you'll see endless fields of golden wheat. Some people say it looks like a waving sea of gold. Kansas is one of America's top farming states. Farmland and pastures for grazing cattle cover most of the state.

No other state grows more wheat or **mills** more wheat into food products than Kansas. It is the leader in grain sorghum, which is used for cattle feed. It is also the leader for the production of ethanol, which is added to gasoline for cars and trucks. However, beef cattle bring in the most farm income. Kansas farmers also raise soybeans, hay, hogs, sunflowers, and dairy cattle.

Many Kansas farm goods end up in factories that produce several of the packaged foods you see in the grocery store. Wheat mills grind wheat into flour. Meat-packing plants cut and package beef. Other farm products are made into baby food and pet food.

▲ **A pig cools off in the mud on a farm in east-central Kansas.**

▲ **Pizza Hut is one of the major fast food restaurants that got its start in Kansas.**

Speaking of food, don't forget fast food! The first White Castle hamburger restaurant opened in Wichita in 1921. Pizza Hut began in Kansas, too. Now it's the world's largest pizza restaurant chain. Big Cheese Pizza, Taco Tico, and Taco Grande also got their start in Kansas.

Airplanes and airplane equipment are Kansas's top factory products. Wichita is called the Air Capital of the World. Its factories make both military and regular aircraft. Wichita produces more nonmilitary airplanes than any city in the world. Other factories make cars, railroad cars, farm machines, and tires.

▲ Helium inside these balloons is what makes them rise into the air.

Have you ever watched a balloon float up in the air? It rises because it has helium inside. Helium is a gas that's lighter than oxygen. That's why it rises. Kansas produces more helium than any other state. However, petroleum and natural gas are Kansas's top mining products. Zinc, salt, and chalk are some other Kansas minerals.

Service industries bring in the most state income. Kansas's service businesses include stores, restaurants, banks, hospitals, and schools. Truck drivers and people with jobs at Kansas's military bases are service workers. Teachers, store clerks, and computer programmers are service workers, too. They all use their skills to make life better for others.

Manufacturing provides almost as much state income as service industries. Farming and ranching make up a smaller part of the state income than either services or manufacturing.

▲ **A farm south of Argonia in Sumner County**

Getting to Know Kansans

One hundred years ago, most Kansans lived on farms. Today, most live in or near big cities. Kansas had 2,694,641 residents in 2001. That made it thirty-second in population among all the states.

Wichita is Kansas's largest city. Next in size is Overland Park, a suburb of Kansas City. More people live in this suburb than in Kansas City itself! Kansas City is the third-largest city. It's right across the border from Kansas City, Missouri, which is that state's largest city. Topeka, the state capital, ranks fourth in population. Western Kansas is very thinly populated.

Native Americans were the first people to settle Kansas. By 1860, most of these native people were displaced by pioneers from the eastern states. Also, **immigrants** arrived from Russia, Germany, Sweden, Italy, and other European countries. African-Americans lived in early Kansas, too. Some were free, while others started out as slaves. Today, about eighteen out of twenty residents are white. About one out of twenty residents is African-American. Asian, Native American, and **Hispanic** people live in Kansas, as well.

▲ **Performers in a Swedish dance at a parade during Svensk Hyllningsfest**

Lindsborg holds a Swedish festival called Svensk Hyllnings-fest. It celebrates Swedish pioneer days with food, costumes, dances, and crafts. Wilson hosts a Czech festival, and Topeka celebrates the Mexican Fiesta. Native Americans hold powwows in several cities. They celebrate their **culture** with dance contests, food, and crafts.

State and county fairs are big events. Hutchinson hosts the Kansas State Fair every September. People show off their prize crops and farm animals. They also enjoy music, food, and rodeos. Abilene holds the Central Kansas Free Fair in August.

Imagine crowds of women racing down the street flipping pancakes in their skillets. That's what happens on International Pancake Day in Liberal. Not only is this happening in Liberal—women in Olney, England, are doing the same thing at the same time! The two towns race each other on Shrove Tuesday. That's the day before the pre-Easter season of Lent begins.

▲ **Women run with pancake skillets during the International Pancake Race in Liberal.**

▲ **Hattie McDaniel (right) with actress Vivien Leigh in a scene from *Gone with the Wind***

Kansas gave us many beloved actors, musicians, and writers. One is actor Kirstie Alley, from the television show *Cheers.* Others are the famous clown Emmett Kelley and the silent-movie comic Buster Keaton. Hattie McDaniel appeared in *Gone with the Wind* (1939). She was the first African-American to win an Academy Award.

▲ **Charlie Parker was a famous jazz musician from Kansas who played the saxophone.**

Jazz musicians Charlie "Bird" Parker and Stan Kenton came from Kansas. Poets Gwendolyn Brooks and Edgar Lee Masters did, too. They all make Kansans proud of their state and their people.

Let's Explore Kansas!

▲ **Front Street in Dodge City**

Many visitors love Kansas for its Wild West **heritage.** They head straight for Dodge City. The famous lawmen Wyatt Earp and Bat Masterson kept order there. Unlucky outlaws ended up in Boot Hill Cemetery. Today, the Boot Hill Museum stands where that cemetery used to be. New buildings that look just like those from the Wild West days line Front Street.

Abilene was another cow town. In Old Abilene Town, you can hop aboard a stagecoach for a bumpy tour of the area.

Abilene was also the boyhood home of President Dwight D. Eisenhower. Today, visitors can see his home and his presidential library and museum.

Tall grasses once covered the Great Plains. Little by little, settlers cleared the grasses for farms and towns. Now Tallgrass Prairie National Preserve protects thousands of acres of native grasslands. This is the largest stretch of tallgrass prairie remaining in North America.

Take a look at a stick of chalk. Did you know chalk is a type of limestone? It's formed from the shells of tiny water

▲ Native grassland is protected at the Tallgrass Prairie National Preserve.

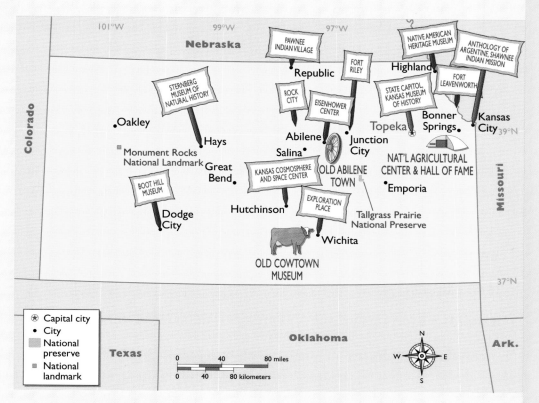

Places to visit in Kansas

creatures. Western Kansas has some of the biggest chalk beds in the world. Buried in the chalk are thousands of **fossils.** They are the remains of fish, reptiles, and birds that lived millions of years ago.

You can look at many of those fossils at the Sternberg Museum of Natural History in Hays. You'll also see huge dinosaurs and the famous "fish-within-a-fish." That's a fossil fish whose stomach contains a fish it ate!

More ancient rock formations await you at Rock City. This site is full of giant, rounded sandstone rocks. Near Oakley, tall rocks tower above the plains. They are Monument Rocks and are sometimes called the Chalk Pyramids.

The state capitol stands in Topeka. It was modeled after the U.S. Capitol in Washington, D.C. Topeka is also home to the Kansas Museum of History. There, you'll see hundreds of historic exhibits. These include a Cheyenne tepee, a covered wagon, a railroad train from the frontier days, and a 1950s diner.

Wichita is Kansas's airplane-making center. At Wichita's

▲ **Boulders at Rock City**

Exploration Place, you'll learn about travel as well as some interesting facts about the environment. Not far from Wichita is Hutchinson, where the Cosmosphere and Space Center contains real space suits and spacecraft.

Many historic forts remain in Kansas. Fort Riley is near Junction City. It was a famous center for the U.S. cavalry, or horseback troops. You'll learn about them at Fort Riley's cavalry museum. Fort Scott was another cavalry post. Fort Leavenworth was the first permanent white settlement in Kansas. Today, the fort houses a college for U.S. Army officers as well as a prison.

▲ An exhibit at Exploration Place in Wichita

Anthology of Argentine is the name of a gigantic work of art in Kansas City. It's a mural, or wall painting, that's 660 feet (201 meters) long. In vivid colors, it shows the area's history from prehistoric times until today.

▲ **The Native American Heritage Center in Highland preserves Native American history and culture.**

The National Agricultural Center and Hall of Fame is in Bonner Springs near Kansas City. Shawnee Indian Mission is close to Kansas City, too. The Native American Heritage Museum is in Highland. It explores the cultures of Kansas's Iowa, Kickapoo, Potawatomi, and Sac and Fox people.

Pawnee Indian Village State Historic Site is near Republic. Along the village's walking trail are earth lodges and storage pits. In the museum, you'll see a Pawnee sacred bundle. This collection of objects was used in planting and harvesting ceremonies.

Kansas has an exciting history and is filled with places to visit and new wonders to discover. You're sure to agree that the Sunflower State is a great state to explore!

Important Dates

1541 Spanish explorer Francisco Vásquez de Coronado crosses present-day Kansas.

1803 The land that will later be Kansas becomes part of the United States in the Louisiana Purchase.

1850s Kansas is called "Bleeding Kansas" because of fights over slavery.

1854 The Territory of Kansas is established.

1861 Kansas becomes the thirty-fourth U.S. state on January 29.

1894 Oil and natural gas are first pumped from Kansas fields.

1905 Helium is discovered near Dexter.

1934–1935 Dust storms devastate Kansas farmland.

1952 Kansan Dwight D. Eisenhower is elected president of the United States; he is reelected in 1956.

1991 Joan Finney becomes Kansas's first woman governor.

1996 Former Kansas senator Robert Dole runs for president of the United States but loses to Bill Clinton.

2002 A bronze statue of a Native American named Ad Astra is mounted atop the capitol. This officially completes the building more than one hundred years after its construction.

Glossary

culture—a group of people's beliefs, customs, and way of life

fossils—forms left in stone by ancient plants and animals

heritage—things of value that are passed down to later people

hides—the skins of an animal

Hispanic—people of Mexican, South American, and other Spanish-speaking cultures

immigrants—people who come to another country to live

industry—a business or trade

irrigation—a method of bringing water to crops

mills—grinds up using special machinery

pioneers—people who explore or settle in a new land

topsoil—the top layer of soil, usually richer than the soil underneath

Did You Know?

★ The name *Kansas* comes from the Sioux Indian word *Kansa,* meaning "people of the south wind." This was what the Sioux called the Kaw, or Kansa, Indians.

★ One bushel of Kansas wheat makes about 42 loaves of white bread (1.5 pounds/.68 kilograms each) or 90 loaves of whole wheat bread (1 lb./.45 kg each).

★ In Kansas, the Arkansas River is pronounced "ar-KAN-zas." It's pronounced "AR-kan-saw" in the other states it passes through.

★ Kansas's grain elevators are called Prairie Skyscrapers.

★ In 1887, Susanna Salter was elected mayor of Argonia. She was the first woman mayor in the United States.

At a Glance

State capital: Topeka

State motto: *Ad Astra per Aspera* (Latin for "To the Stars Through Difficulties")

State nickname: Sunflower State

Statehood: January 29, 1861; thirty-fourth state

Land area: 81,823 square miles (211,922 square kilometers); **rank:** thirteenth

Highest point: Mount Sunflower, 4,039 feet (1,232 meters) above sea level

Lowest point: Along the Verdigris River in Montgomery County, 680 feet (207 m) above sea level

Highest recorded temperature: 121°F (49°C) at Fredonia on July 18, 1936, and near Alton on July 24, 1936

Lowest recorded temperature: −40°F (−40°C) at Lebanon on February 13, 1905

Average January temperature: 30°F (−1°C)

Average July temperature: 78°F (26°C)

Population in 2001: 2,694,641; **rank:** thirty-second

Largest cities in 2000: Wichita (344,284), Overland Park (149,080), Kansas City (146,866), Topeka (122,377)

Factory products: Transportation equipment, food products, machines

Farm products: Wheat, beef cattle, corn, sorghum, soybeans

Mining products: Petroleum, natural gas, helium

State flag: Kansas's state flag features  the state seal upon a blue background. Above the seal is a sunflower, the state flower. A bar of twisted gold and blue is beneath the sunflower. Below the seal is the word *Kansas* in gold letters.

State seal: The state seal shows many symbols of nature, history, and industry in Kansas. The sun rising over a mountain represents the east, where most of Kansas's early settlers came from. A steamboat on a river represents trade. A settler's cabin and a man plowing stand for Kansas's agriculture. A line of covered wagons stands for pioneers' westward journey. Native Americans pursue a herd of buffalo, representing Kansas's past as a Native American homeland. At the top of the seal is the state motto. Beneath it, a cluster of thirty-four stars stands for Kansas's place as the thirty-fourth state.

State abbreviations: Kans. or Kan. (traditional); KS (postal)

State Symbols

State bird: Western meadowlark

State flower: Wild native sunflower

State tree: Cottonwood

State mammal: American buffalo (bison)

State reptile: Ornate box turtle

State amphibian: Barred tiger salamander

State insect: Honeybee

State soil: Harney silt loam

Making Whole Wheat Bread-Crumb Pancakes

Kansas wheat products make delicious pancakes!

Makes eight 4-inch pancakes.

INGREDIENTS:

1 ½ cups whole wheat bread crumbs

1 ¼ cups low-fat milk

1 tablespoon vegetable oil

1 egg, beaten

½ cup flour

2 teaspoons baking powder

DIRECTIONS:

Make sure an adult helps you with the hot skillet. Using your hands or a blender, shred the bread into very small crumbs. Put them in a bowl with the milk until they're soft. It will take just a few minutes. Add the oil and egg and mix well. In another bowl, mix the flour and baking powder together. Add this to the bread-crumb mixture and stir just until it's all blended. If it's too thick, add a little more milk. Heat a skillet over medium heat. Pour in about ¼ cup of the batter. Cook until bubbles begin to form on the top of the pancake. Turn it over, and cook the other side. Repeat until you've used up all the batter.

Serve with margarine or your favorite toppings.

"Home on the Range"

Words by Dr. Brewster Higley, music by Daniel Kelly
(The words of the official version are not quite the same as other, more familiar, versions.)

Oh, give me a home where the buffalo roam,
Where the deer and the antelope play,
Where seldom is heard a discouraging word
And the sky is not clouded all day.

Chorus:
A home, a home where the deer and the
antelope play,
Where seldom is heard a discouraging word
And the sky is not clouded all day.

Oh, give me the gale of the Solomon vale,
Where life streams with buoyancy flow,
On the banks of the Beaver, where seldom
if ever
Any poisonous herbage doth grow.

Oh, give me the land where the bright
diamond sand
Throws its light from the glittering stream
Where glideth along the graceful white swan,
Like a maid in a heavenly dream.

I love the wild flowers in the bright land
of ours;
I love too the wild curley's scream
The bluffs and white rocks and antelope flocks
That graze on the hillsides so green.

How often at night, when the heavens
are bright
With the light of the glittering stars,
Have I stood here amazed and asked as
I gazed
If their glory exceeds this of ours.

The air is so pure, the breezes so free,
The zephyrs so balmy and light,
I would not exchange my home here
to range
Forever in azure so bright.

Kirstie Alley (1955–) is an actress. She became famous for her role in the television series *Cheers.* Alley was born in Wichita.

Gwendolyn Brooks (1917–2000) was the first African-American to win a Pulitzer Prize. She won it for her poetry collection *Annie Allen* (1949). Brooks was born in Topeka.

Walter Chrysler (1875–1940) was a car-maker. He founded the Chrysler Corporation in 1925. Chrysler was born in Wamego.

Charles Curtis (1860–1936) was the first person of Native American ancestry to serve as U.S. vice president (1929–1933). He was born in Topeka.

Robert Dole (1923–) is a politician. He served as a U.S. senator (1969–1996) from Kansas. He ran for president in 1996, losing to Bill Clinton. Dole was born in Russell.

Amelia Earhart (1897–1937?) was the first woman to fly solo across the Atlantic Ocean (1932). She was born in Atchison.

Dwight D. Eisenhower (1890–1969) led the Allies' invasion of Europe in World War II. He was the thirty-fourth U.S. president (1953–1961). Born in Texas, he grew up in Abilene.

Melissa Etheridge (1961–) is a popular singer and guitarist. She was born in Leavenworth.

Dennis Hopper (1936–) is a movie actor and director. He was born in Dodge City.

William Inge (1913–1973) wrote plays, including *Come Back, Little Sheba* (1950), which was made into a movie. He was born in Independence.

Buster Keaton (1895–1966) was a comic actor who first appeared in silent movies. He was born in Piqua.

Emmett Kelly (1898–1979) was a famous circus clown. He was born in Sedan.

Stan Kenton (1912–1979) was a jazz musician and bandleader. He was born in Wichita.

Edgar Lee Masters (1869–1950) was a poet. His most famous poetry collection is *Spoon River Anthology* (1915). Masters was born in Garnett.

Hattie McDaniel (1895–1952) was the first African-American to win an Academy Award. She won it for her role as Mammy in *Gone with the Wind* (1939). McDaniel was born in Wichita.

Charlie Parker (1920–1955) was a jazz saxophone player who inspired many musicians. His nickname was "Bird." Parker (pictured above left) was born in Kansas City.

Gordon Parks (1912–) is a film director. He was born in Fort Scott.

Damon Runyon (1884–1946) was a short-story writer. His collection *Guys and Dolls* (1931) was made into a Broadway play and was later a movie. Runyon was born in Manhattan.

Want to Know More?

At the Library

Brenner, Barbara, and Don Bolognese (illustrator). *Wagon Wheels.* New York: HarperCollins, 1993.

Garretson, Jerri, and Diane Dollar (illustrator). *Johnny Kaw: The Pioneer Spirit of Kansas.* Manhattan, Kan.: Ravenstone Press, 1997.

Ingram, Scott. *Kansas.* Danbury, Conn.: Children's Press, 2003.

Osborne, Mary Pope, and Sal Murdocca (illustrator). *Twister on Tuesday.* New York: Random House, 2001.

Shannon, George, and Thomas B. Allen (illustrator). *Climbing Kansas Mountains.* New York: Bradbury Press, 1993.

Welsbacher, Anne. *Kansas.* Edina, Minn.: Abdo & Daughters, 1998.

On the Web
For more information on this topic, use FactHound.

1. Go to *www.facthound.com*
2. Type in this book ID: 0756503531
3. Click on the *Fetch It* button.

FactHound will find the best Web sites for you.

Through the Mail
accessKansas

Information Network of Kansas, Inc.
534 South Kansas Avenue, Suite 1210
Topeka, KS 66603
For general information about Kansas

Department of Travel and Tourism

Kansas Department of Commerce and Housing
1000 S.W. Jackson, Suite 100
Topeka, KS 66612
For information on travel and recreation in Kansas

On the Road
Kansas History Center

6425 S.W. Sixth Avenue
Topeka, KS 66615
785/272-8681
To see fascinating exhibits on Kansas history

Kansas State Capitol

300 S.W. 10th Street
Topeka, KS 66612
785/296-3966
To visit Kansas's state capitol

Index

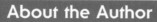

About the Author

Ann Heinrichs grew up in Fort Smith, Arkansas, and lives in Chicago. She is the author of more than one hundred books for children and young adults on Asian, African, and U.S. history and culture. Ann has also written numerous newspaper, magazine, and encyclopedia articles. She is an award-winning martial artist, specializing in t'ai chi empty-hand and sword forms.

Ann has traveled widely throughout the United States, Africa, Asia, and the Middle East. In exploring each state for this series, she rediscovered the people, history, and resources that make this a great land, as well as the concerns we share with people around the world.

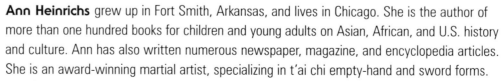